Digestion
and
Nutrition

What Happens to the Food We Eat?

Eve Hartman and Wendy Meshbesher

Raintree

Chicago, Illinois

Edited by Adam Miller, Sian Smith, and Penny West
Designed by Philippa Jenkins
Original illustrations © Capstone Global Library Ltd 2014
Illustrated by Medi-mation
Picture research by Tracy Cummins
Originated by Capstone Global Library Ltd
Produced by Victoria Fitzgerald
Printed and bound in China by CTPS

17 16 15 14 13
10 9 8 7 6 5 4 3 2 1

Library of Congress Cataloging-in-Publication Data
Hartman, Eve.
 Digestion and nutrition : what happens to the food we eat? / Eve Hartman and Wendy Meshbesher.
  pages cm.—(Show me science)
 Includes bibliographical references and index.
 ISBN 978-1-4329-8748-0 (hb)—ISBN 978-1-4329-8755-8 (pb) 1. Digestion—Juvenile literature. 2. Digestive organs—Juvenile literature. 3. Gastrointestinal system—Juvenile literature. 4. Nutrition—Juvenile literature. I. Meshbesher, Wendy. II. Title.

QP145.H37 2014
612.3—dc23   2013013103

Acknowledgments
The author and publisher are grateful to the following for permission to reproduce copyright material:
Corbis p. 27 (© David Mbiyu / Demotix); Getty Images pp. 9 top (Peter Carroll), 10 (BSIP/UIG), 11 (George Doyle), 21 (Museum of the City of New York/Byron Collection), 23 (Albert L. Ortega/WireImage); Newscom pp. 4 (Sharkpixs / ZUMAPRESS.com), 24 (Steve Russell/The Toronto Star/ZUMAPRESS.com); Shutterstock pp. 5 (© Giuseppe_R), 8 (© Timothy Craig Lubcke), 9 bottom (© Monkey Business Images), 13 (© Dorottya Mathe), 14 (© Ulrich Mueller), 17 (© frantisekhojdysz), 19 (© Scorpp), 20 (© sevenke), 26 (© wavebreakmedia), 28 (© Morgan Lane Photography); Superstock pp. 6 (Photo Library), 12 (GILLES / BSIP), 15 (Chua Wee Boo / age footstock), 25 (Blend Images / SuperStock); USDA p.18 (content adapted from ChooseMyPlate.gov with thanks to USDA's Center for Nutrition Policy and Promotion).

Cover photograph reproduced with permission of Getty Images (Stockbyte).

We would like to thank Ann Fullick for her invaluable help in the preparation of this book.

Every effort has been made to contact copyright holders of any material reproduced in this book. Any omissions will be rectified in subsequent printings if notice is given to the publisher.

On Your Marks... Get Set... 4

The Digestive System 6

The Mouth 8

Esophagus and Stomach 10

The Intestines 12

Grass for Food?! 14

Where Does Food Go? 16

A Balanced Diet 18

Protein Foods 20

Fruits and Vegetables 22

Dairy 24

Sharing Meals 26

Summary 28

Quiz 29

Glossary 30

Find Out More 31

Index 32

Some words are shown in bold, **like this**. You can find out what they mean by looking in the glossary.

On Your Marks...
Get Set...

GO! But this racer is not running. He is eating hot dogs! After 10 minutes, the person who eats the most hot dogs is the winner.

At the hot dog-eating contest, cards show how many hot dogs a contestant has eaten.

Contest strategy and rules

Most contestants dip the buns in water, which helps them to swallow them quickly. Ketchup and mustard are allowed, but most do not bother with this. The hot dog and the bun must be swallowed for the hot dog to count.

The Nathan's Hot Dog-Eating Contest is held at Coney Island in New York City on July 4 every year. Piles of hot dogs are set in front of the contestants. In 2013, the men's winner was Joey Chestnut. He broke his own record, eating 69 hot dogs! His prizes included money, a trophy, and...two boxes of hot dogs!

Healthy eating

Without practice and training, eating very quickly is not safe or healthy. You could choke or vomit. You might also feel bloated and weak after your meal.

Healthy eating involves a healthy **diet**. A hot dog contains meat and bread, both of which are part of a healthy diet. But it also contains things your body needs only in small amounts, such as fat and salt. Your body needs other **nutrients** that are not found in hot dogs.

We need to eat many different kinds of food. Why? And what happens to food after we eat it? You will find out in this book!

The Digestive System

When you put food in your mouth, you are sending it on a journey into your body. The **digestive system** is the set of body parts, or **organs**, that breaks down food into very small pieces. The mouth is part of this system.

Why does the body need a digestive system? Most of the food we eat is in pieces that are too large for the body to use. Even a breadcrumb is too big! The digestive system breaks down food to release its **nutrients**. Food also contains parts that the body cannot use. These parts leave the body as waste.

What happens to all the food?

Some **digested** food is used to make or develop body parts, such as bones and muscles. A baby girl can grow into a child, and then an adult, because of all the food she eats.

However, the body uses most food for energy. You need energy whenever you move your body and especially when you exercise. You will learn about food and energy on page 16.

TINY HELPERS

The digestive system does not work alone. **Bacteria** are tiny living things. Some bacteria make you sick. But inside the **small intestine**, bacteria help to break down food. Scientists think about 100 trillion live there. But all those bacteria weigh only about 4½ pounds (2 kilograms).

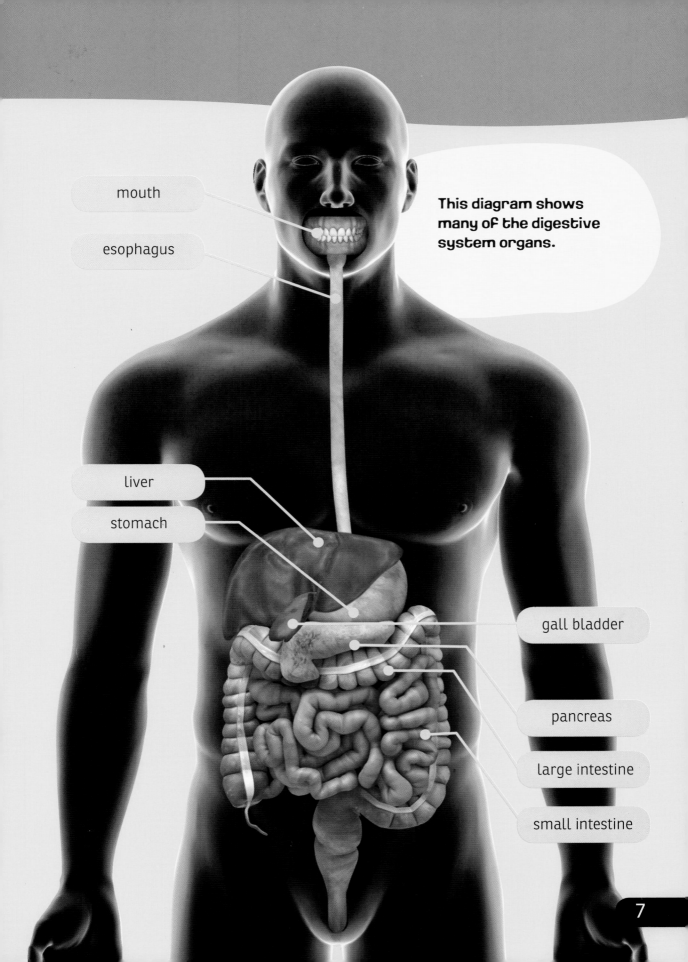

mouth

esophagus

This diagram shows many of the digestive system organs.

liver

stomach

gall bladder

pancreas

large intestine

small intestine

Digestion begins in the mouth. The teeth break down food into smaller pieces. The sharp front teeth cut and slice the food. Flat back teeth, called molars, grind the food.

The mouth also breaks down food **chemically**. This means that it changes the chemicals that are in the food. A liquid called **saliva** causes these changes. The mouth releases saliva just before you start eating. It releases more when you start chewing.

Open wide!

With a mouth this big, a hippopotamus might beat any human in an eating contest! But those big tusks will not help it eat. Hippos use them to pick fights with other hippos. Their teeth for eating are in the back of the mouth. They are much smaller than the tusks.

Around age six, the two upper front teeth are often the first to be pushed out.

Meet your teeth

Teeth are hard and strong. Keeping teeth clean will keep them healthy, and so will visits to the dentist. A young child has 20 teeth. But while the child's mouth grows, the teeth do not. Instead, starting from around the age of six, a new set of 32 teeth push out the old teeth. The second set is called the adult teeth. The body cannot replace adult teeth. They need to last your whole life.

Brushing and flossing will keep your teeth clean and healthy. Visits to the dentist help, too.

After you swallow a piece of food, it travels down a tube called the **esophagus**. Like other parts of the **digestive system**, the esophagus is a tube with muscles in its walls. The muscles push the food along in the right direction. This is why you can eat upside down (if you really have to).

The esophagus leads to the **stomach**, the next **organ** of the digestive system. It is like a bag for holding food. The muscles of the stomach squeeze and churn the food.

The inner walls of the stomach have many folds that expand to hold a large meal.

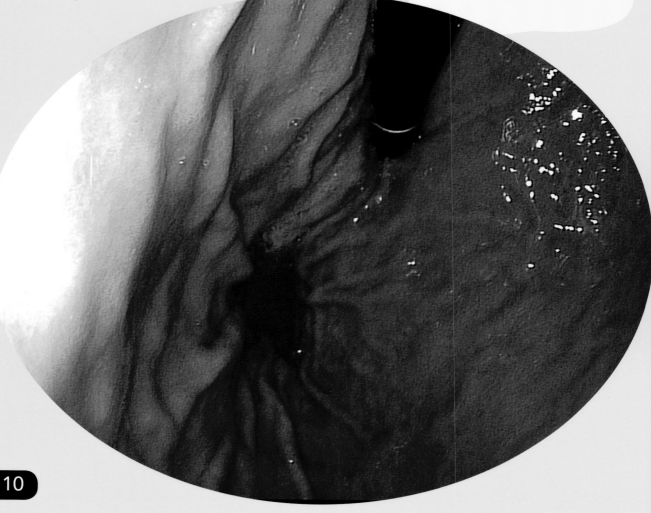

Oops, wrong way!

When you breathe in through your mouth, why does air go to the lungs, while food goes down the esophagus? Like a switch, a flap of skin opens and closes to send air and food down the right tubes. Normally, the flap works very well. But if you try to talk and eat at the same time, food can start to go down the wrong tube. Usually you can cough the food up quickly. But it is not a fun experience!

Stomach acid

The stomach makes strong **acid**. This makes the right conditions for special chemicals to break down the **protein** that you eat. It also kills germs that might have entered with food.

If you have ever vomited, you might have felt the burn of stomach acid in your mouth. So what protects the stomach from its own acid? The stomach is lined with a thick, waxy substance called **mucus**. Acid does not harm it.

The Intestines

After food leaves the **stomach**, it enters the **small intestine**. The small intestine is a narrow tube packed into tight coils. If you could stretch it out, its length would be 22 feet (7 meters). That is about the height of a two-story building.

Remember that the stomach adds **acid** to the food. In the small intestine, juices from other **organs** act to **neutralize** the acid. These juices also cause more chemical changes to the food to break it down further. Much of the food is now in the form of tiny **nutrients**. The nutrients pass through the lining of the small intestine and into the blood.

At the end of the small intestine, any food that remains is passed to the **large intestine**. The large intestine is a short, wide tube. The walls of the large intestine take in water from the food. The remaining food then leaves the body as **feces** (solid waste).

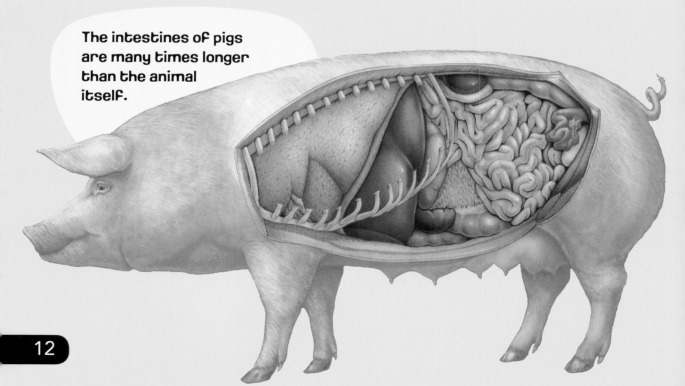

The intestines of pigs are many times longer than the animal itself.

Towel vs. T-shirt

Have you ever cleaned up a spill? A towel will do the job much better than a T-shirt. Look closely at a towel, and you will see lots of thin threads or folds. The threads and folds help to soak up the water. The lining of the small intestine is also bumpy and folded. The lining helps to gather up the nutrients.

Small vs. large

The small intestine is much longer than the large intestine. It is named "small" because it is narrow. The large intestine is wider.

Grass for Food?!

Could you eat grass? No way! Your **digestive system** cannot break down tough plant parts, such as grass, bark, and needles. But grass and other plant parts are good food for cows, sheep, and other grazing animals. They can break down grass because their digestive systems are very long, have many parts, and contain special **bacteria**.

Long intestines and a four-part stomach help a cow digest grass.

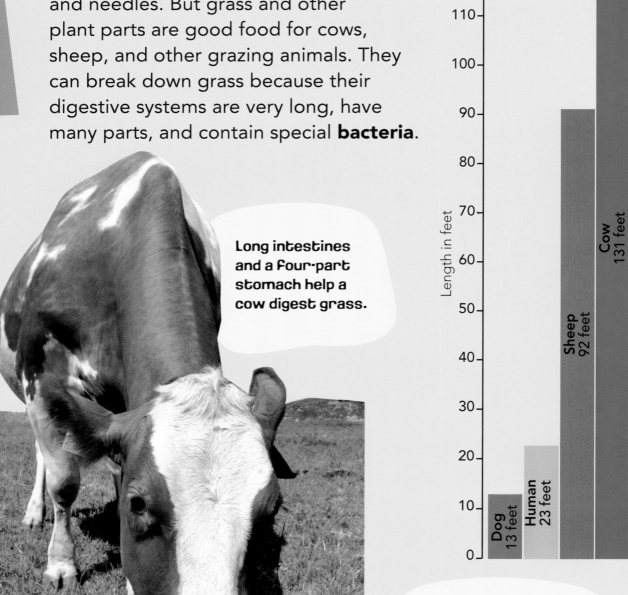

Length in feet

130
120
110
100
90
80
70
60
50
40
30
20
10
0

Dog
13 feet

Human
23 feet

Sheep
92 feet

Cow
131 feet

Compare the length of the **small intestine** in these animals. Do you think dogs could live on grass?

Cows and birds

A cow's **stomach** is divided into four parts. Food spends time in each part and returns to the mouth in a partly **digested** form, called cud. Cows chew the cud, then swallow it again. Goats, sheep, and horses have stomachs like this, too.

Have you ever seen a bird swallow a small stone? Birds use stones to help digest their food! They hold the stones in the gizzard, which is like a pouch. The stones act like a set of loose teeth to mash the food.

The wood eaters

While cows and sheep can eat grass, they cannot digest wood. That is a job for much smaller animals, such as termites (antlike insects). Termites often live in warm, wet forests.

Termites can eat wood because of **protists** that live in their guts. Protists are very small living things that usually live in the soil or water. The protists that live in termites make chemicals that help break down wood.

Termites are pests in people's homes, but fill an important role in nature.

Where Does Food Go?

What happens to **nutrients** after they leave the **digestive system**? They enter the blood, which carries them all around the body.

The human body is made of tiny parts called **cells**. Blood takes nutrients to all body cells. Some nutrients help cells grow or make new parts. Other nutrients are used for energy.

To use this energy, cells need **oxygen**. The lungs take in oxygen, and blood takes oxygen to the cells. The oxygen is used to break down the nutrients even more. Finally the nutrients can be used as energy.

This process releases a waste gas called **carbon dioxide**. Your body gets rid of carbon dioxide when you breathe air out of your lungs. When you breathe out carbon dioxide, you are saying goodbye to food you ate!

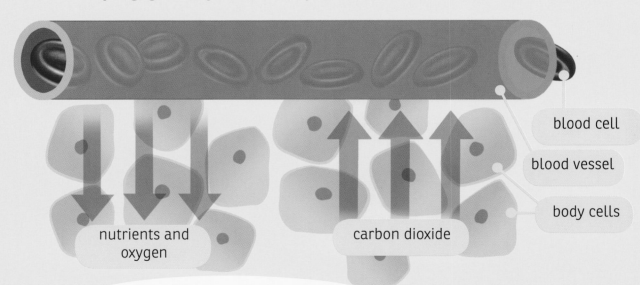

nutrients and oxygen

carbon dioxide

blood cell

blood vessel

body cells

Nutrients and oxygen move through the blood vessel walls to the cells. Carbon dioxide is produced and taken away in the blood.

Storing food

The body has many ways to store food. Making fat is one of these ways. You can live on stored food for a few days. However, the body cannot store gases. This is why you must breathe in and out every few seconds, even when you are asleep. Testing the body's limits is very dangerous. Each story described in the chart below almost ended in death.

Surviving without basic needs

Need	Recommended	Without it, death usually occurs after	Extreme story
Food	Three balanced meals a day	Three weeks	Hiker James Scott was lost in snowy mountains. He lived for 43 days without eating.
Water	Eight glasses (48 ounces / 1.5 liters) a day	Three days	Mountain hiker Mitsutaka Uchikoshi lived 24 days without food or water.
Air	A breath every few seconds	Two to three minutes	Deep-sea diver Tom Sietas held his breath for 22 minutes, 22 seconds.

Divers can stay underwater until their oxygen tanks are empty.

A Balanced Diet

No single food—not even hot dogs!—provides all the **nutrients** that the body needs. This is why it is important to eat a balanced **diet** that includes many different kinds of foods.

Starchy foods

Starchy foods, such as potatoes, provide most of the body's energy, because they are made mostly of **carbohydrates**. Carbohydrates are nutrients rich in energy.

Grains are a group of plants that include wheat, corn, rice, and oats. We eat only a small part, called the **kernel**, of these plants. The kernels are used to make flour, which is baked into bread, pasta, and cereal.

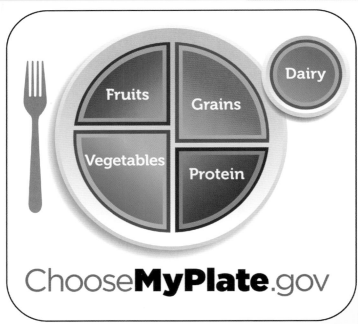

ChooseMyPlate.gov

The MyPlate above shows how much of what you eat should come from each **food group**.

Whole-grain foods, like these breads, provide more **vitamins** and fiber than other grain products.

Grains also contain **fiber**, tough plant material that the body cannot break down. But fiber is useful because it helps to keep food moving through the **digestive system**.

To get the most benefit from grains, eat whole-grain foods. They contain the whole grain kernel. Brown rice, popcorn, and oatmeal are whole-grain foods. Some flour is whole-grain, too. Eat only small amounts of grain foods that contain extra sugar or fat.

A champion of many foods

In 2005, Sonya Thomas of Alexandria, Virginia, won a popcorn-eating contest by eating 10 boxes in 12 minutes. Popcorn is only one of her favorite foods. She holds world records for eating hamburgers, crab cakes, crayfish, eggs, and fruitcake. Remember, though, this is not healthy eating!

19

Protein Foods

Proteins are **nutrients** that help the body live, grow, and repair itself. Foods rich in proteins make up the protein **food group**. This includes meat from all kinds of animals, including chicken and fish. Eggs are part of the protein group, too.

Beans, nuts, and seeds are foods from plants that are rich in proteins. Peanut butter is a good source of protein. When you eat a sandwich of natural peanut butter and whole-grain bread, you are getting grains and proteins. Add some carrots, fruit, and a glass of milk, and you have a healthy lunch.

Beans are a useful source of protein.

Hot dog history

Hot dogs are sometimes called frankfurters, because they first became popular in the city of Frankfurt, Germany. People disagree on the exact date and place the first hot dog was made, but they spread all over the world. In 1916, Nathan Handwerker of Poland opened a hot dog stand in New York City. On July 4 that year, the stand held its first hot dog-eating contest. The contest has been held almost every year since.

The first hot dog stands in the United States opened over 100 years ago. People have been lining up ever since!

No meat, please

Some people choose not to eat meat. Others avoid all foods that come from animals, including milk and eggs. If you avoid certain foods, make sure you still eat a balanced **diet**. Eating beans, nuts, and seeds can give your body the protein and other important nutrients it needs.

Fruits and vegetables

All sorts of plants make fruits and vegetables that are good to eat. You could eat three new fruits every day, for a whole year! Even then, there would still be more fruits to try.

Fruits and vegetables provide the body with many of the **vitamins** it needs. Vitamins are **nutrients** the body uses only in small amounts. The body needs vitamins to live and grow properly. Many fruits are sweet and tasty. They make great desserts and snacks. Fruits and vegetables also provide **fiber**.

Food festivals

Who throws parties for fruits and vegetables? People around the world, that's who. The chart opposite shows some examples.

A free dinner...for the very hungry!

The big Texan Restaurant offers very hungry people a steak dinner for no charge. But there is a catch. The dinner is huge, and diners have to eat all of it in one hour or otherwise they pay! The steak weighs 4½ pounds (2 kilograms). That is about the same weight as 18 hamburger patties. For most people, eating a huge steak dinner in a very short time is not healthy. Remember, you should always stop eating when you feel full.

Town	Festival food	Dishes to try
Alresford, United Kingdom	watercress	watercress soup
Aarau, Switzerland	carrots	carrot cake
Benicarlo, Spain	artichokes	barbecued artichokes
Gilroy, California	garlic	garlic ice cream
Kapaa, Hawaii	coconuts	coconut pie
Pershore, United Kingdom	plums	plum custard
Pasedena, California	watermelon	watermelon slices
Trevi, Italy	black celery	celery with cheese or olive oil

The dairy group includes milk and food made with milk, such as cheese, yogurt, and ice cream. Dairy foods are important because they provide **calcium**. Dairy products also are rich in **vitamin** D. The body uses both calcium and vitamin D to make strong bones and teeth.

Many dairy foods include fat. Ice cream and frozen yogurt have sugar added to them. Be careful about getting too much fat and sugar in your **diet**. They can provide more energy than your body needs and can lead to gaining weight.

In some countries, butter sculptures are popular exhibits at fairs and festivals.

Food for infants

The **digestive system** of a newborn baby cannot break down most foods. The best food for babies is milk from their mothers. This milk provides all the **nutrients** that a young baby needs to live and grow. If this is not available, special formulas can mimic this milk, too. After a few months, the baby can begin eating solid food. Before long, a young child may eat most foods that adults eat.

Feeding time is special for both mothers and babies.

The story of cheese

People have been making cheese for at least 5,000 years. The ancient Greeks made cheese, and cheese-making is in some of their stories and legends. But who invented cheese? According to one story, an Arab man stored some milk in a pouch. The pouch was made from the **stomach** of a sheep. Chemicals from the stomach and warm temperatures changed part of the milk into cheese. He was a brave man to try that first cheese!

Sharing Meals

Food experts say that you should eat three meals a day: breakfast, lunch, and dinner. Each meal should include a variety of foods that make up a balanced **diet**.

However, eating is about more than just food. Eating is also a social event, meaning people enjoy it together. During lunchtime at school, friends share jokes or stories. At dinnertime, families share a meal and discuss their day.

Let's celebrate!

Meals also help people to celebrate. They are often part of birthday parties, festivals, and weddings. Many holidays involve special foods or meals.

What are some favorite meals you have enjoyed? Was the food the most important part of the meal? What else made the meal memorable?

A good meal is even better when it is shared.

Braai Day in South Africa

Every year on September 24, the people of South Africa celebrate Braai Day. Braai is a kind of barbecue. Native Africans invented the braai style of cooking meat. Today, Braai Day helps unite all the people of South Africa.

Some holidays, like Braai Day, are all about the food!

Hot dogs and other food are broken down by the **digestive system**. **Digestion** begins in the mouth. Then food travels to the **stomach** and intestines. In the **small intestine**, tiny food particles travel into the blood. The particles are **nutrients** the body uses for energy and to grow.

No single food provides all the nutrients the body needs. A healthy **diet** is called a balanced diet because it includes many kinds of foods. Grains, **protein** foods, fruits, vegetables, and dairy foods together make up a balanced diet.

1

The digestion of a hot dog begins in the:

A. mouth
B. esophagus
C. stomach
D. small intestine

(See page 8)

2

Compared to the large intestine, the small intestine is:

A. shorter
B. narrower
C. straighter
D. wider

(See page 13)

3

Termites can eat wood because of:

A. a four-chambered stomach
B. stones in their gizzards
C. acid that their stomachs make
D. protists that live in their guts

(See page 15)

4

Protein foods are:

A. beans, nuts, and seeds
B. fruits and vegetables
C. whole-grain foods
D. dairy foods

(See page 20)

5

A food rich in calcium and vitamin D is:

A. hot dogs
B. potatoes
C. apples
D. milk

(See page 24)

(Answers: 1A; 2B; 3D; 4A; 5D)

acid chemical in the stomach that helps prepare food for digestion

bacteria tiny, single-celled living thing

calcium mineral needed for healthy bones and teeth

carbohydrate substance that is a source of energy in food

carbon dioxide often a waste gas in a body process, also found in the air

cell tiny unit that all living things are made out of

chemically to do with chemicals—substances that things are made from

diet meal plan—the various different things that a person eats

digest, digestion process of breaking down food into small chemicals that are useful to the body

digestive system system that breaks down food into useful substances that can be used in the body

esophagus muscular tube that carries food to the stomach

feces solid waste from the digestive system, also known as "poop"

fiber tough plant material that passes through the digestive system

food group group of foods that provide similar nutrients

kernel grain or seed

large intestine wide tube near the end of the digestive system

mucus thick, slippery liquid that coats the stomach

neutralize react with something to make it neutral

nutrient important substance taken in by an animal or plant

organ body part that does a specific job

oxygen gas that is part of the air; it is needed by all plants and animals

protein material that is the building block for making the parts of living things, such as muscles and nerves

protist tiny living thing

saliva fluid in the mouth that helps digest food

small intestine long, thin tube where food is digested into nutrients

stomach muscular sack that holds and digests food

vitamin nutrient that the body needs only in small amounts

Find Out More

Books

Gibbons, Gail. *The Vegetables We Eat.* New York: Holiday House, 2008.

Mayo Clinic. *The Mayo Clinic Kids' Cookbook: 50 Favorite Recipes for Fun and Healthy Eating.* Intercourse, Pa: Good Books, 2012.

Pollan, Michael. *The Omnivore's Dilemma: The Secrets Behind What You Eat,* Young Readers Edition. New York: Dial, 2009.

Schlosser, Charles. *Chew on This: Everything You Don't Want to Know About Fast Food.* Boston: Houghton-Mifflin, 2007.

Taylor-Butler, Christine. *The Digestive System* (True Book). New York: Children's Press, 2008.

Web sites

www.choosemyplate.gov
This web site tells you all about healthy eating. Watch videos, make a daily food plan, and learn about each of the food groups.

www.hot-dog.org
Visit Hot Dog City online to learn lots of unusual and interesting facts about hot dogs.

www.nathansfamous.com
Learn more about the history of the hot dog and Nathan's Hot Dog-Eating Contest.

acid 11, 12

babies 25
bacteria 6, 14
balanced diet 5, 18, 21, 26, 28
barbecues 27
beans 20, 21
birds 15
blood 16
Braai Day 27
breathing 16, 17
brushing and flossing teeth 9

calcium 24
capillary walls 16
carbohydrates 18
carbon dioxide 16
cells 16
cheese 25
chemical changes 8, 12
chewing 8
choking 5, 11
cows 14, 15
cud 15

dairy foods 24–25, 28
digestive system 6, 14, 16, 19, 25, 28
divers 17

eating quickly 5, 22
energy 6, 16, 18, 24
esophagus 7, 10, 11
exercise 6

fat 5, 17, 19, 24
feces 12
fiber 19, 23
food festivals 23
food groups 18, 20
food-eating contests 4–5, 19
fruits and vegetables 22–23, 28

gall bladder 7
germs 11
gizzard 15
goats 15
grains 18–19, 20, 28
grass 14
grazing animals 14–15
growth and development 6

hippos 8
horses 15
hot dogs 21
hot-dog contests 4–5, 21

intestines 6, 7, 12–13, 14, 28

large intestine 7, 12, 13
liver 7
lungs 16

milk 24, 25
molars 8
mouth 6, 7, 8–9
mucus 11
muscles 6, 10

nutrients 5, 6, 12, 16, 18, 21, 23, 25, 28
nuts 20, 21

organs 6, 7, 10, 12
overweight 24
oxygen 16

pancreas 7
pigs 12
proteins 11, 20, 21, 28
protists 15

saliva 8
salt 5
sharing meals 26–27
sheep 15
small intestine 6, 7, 12, 13, 14, 28
starch 18
stomach 7, 10, 11, 14, 15, 25, 28
stomach acid 11, 12
sugar 19, 24

teeth 8–9, 24
termites 15

vitamin D 24
vitamins 23, 24
vomiting 5, 11

waste 6, 12, 16
water 17
whole-grain foods 19, 20